CONTEMPORARY

ATTRACTIONS

BOOK ONE

CONTEMPORARY'S

ATTRACTIONS

BOOK ONE

IT'S COLOSSAL

ETHEL TIERSKY
MAXINE CHERNOFF

CB

CONTEMPORARY
BOOKS

CHICAGO

Library of Congress Cataloging-in-Publication Data

Tiersky, Ethel, 1937–
       It's colossal / Ethel Tiersky.
           p.   cm. — (Attractions ; bk. 1)
       ISBN 0-8092-3688-5
       1. Readers—United States.   2. English language—Textbooks for
    foreign speakers.   3. United States—Civilization—Problems,
    exercises, etc.   I. Title.   II. Series: Tiersky, Ethel, 1937–
    Attractions ; bk. 1.
    PE1127.H5T45   1993
    428.6'4—dc20   93-38855
                                                                        CIP

Acknowledgments
We wish to thank the following for sending us background information, answering
innumerable questions by phone, and, in some cases, supplying photographs for this text.

"Golden Door": Peg Zitko, Director of Public Affairs, The Statue of Liberty–Ellis Island
Foundations, Inc.; Manny Strumpf, Public Affairs Officer, New York City, U.S. Department of
the Interior, National Park Service.

"Sky High": Marci J. Grossman, Manager, Media Relations, Sears, Roebuck, and Co.

"Gateway to the West": Robert Moore, historian; Mark Engler, Chief of Museum Services
and Interpretation; Gary W. Easton, Superintendent, Jefferson National Expansion Memorial.

"Heads of State": Jim Popovich, Division of Interpretation, Mount Rushmore National
Memorial; Rob DeWall, Crazy Horse Memorial.

"History in Stone": Arizona Office of Tourism.

"Disney's World": Margaret Adamic, Contracts Coordinator, The Disney Publishing Group.

Photo Credits
Cover photos: Gateway Arch © Alvis Upitis/The Image Bank, Mount Rushmore © Gerald
Brimacombe/The Image Bank, Sears Tower courtesy of Sears, Roebuck, and Co.; Tom
DeHaven: 2, 42; Rob DeWall: 48, 51; Jefferson National Expansion Memorial/National Park
Service: 33; National Park Service: 28; Tribune Files Photos: 11, 18, 58, 63; UPI/Bettmann: 56

Published by Contemporary Books, Inc.
Two Prudential Plaza, Chicago, Illinois 60601-6790
Manufactured in the United States of America
International Standard Book Number: 0-8092-3688-5
10   9   8   7   6   5   4   3   2

Published simultaneously in Canada by
Fitzhenry & Whiteside
195 Allstate Parkway
Markham, Ontario L3R 4T8
Canada

CONTENTS

TO THE READER

Two men camping overnight in a fold of the Statue of Liberty's robe? A mountain climber dressed as Spider-Man scaling the world's tallest building? An architect designing a prize-winning monument that no one knew how to build? A well-known monument named after an unknown lawyer? These are just a few of the amazing facts you will discover in *It's Colossal*, the first book in the four-book reading series ***Attractions***.

Attractions takes you to some of our nation's most visited sites. Each book contains six stories about famous places, things, and people—and the interesting facts behind them. Along the way, you will be able to check your understanding of what you have read. Each story closes with little-known tidbits about the city and state where the attraction is located.

- *Book One, It's Colossal*, features America's giant points of interest: the Statue of Liberty, Sears Tower, the Gateway Arch, Mount Rushmore, the Grand Canyon, and Walt Disney World.

- *Book Two, Back to the Past*, features sites that have important connections to our nation's past: Plimoth Plantation, the White House, New Orleans, the San Francisco Bay Area, the Vietnam Veterans Memorial, and the commonwealth of Puerto Rico.

- *Book Three, Sun and Games*, features the attractions of six of the country's most popular vacation spots: Las Vegas, Graceland, New Mexico, Hawaii, Hollywood, and Minnesota.

- *Book Four, Birthplaces of Ideas*, features places where some of our nation's most important social ideas and inventions began: philosopher Henry David Thoreau's Walden Pond, aviators Orville and Wilbur Wright's

Kitty Hawk, inventor Thomas Edison's New Jersey, civil rights leader Martin Luther King Jr.'s Center for Nonviolent Social Change, architect Frank Lloyd Wright's Taliesin, and conservationist Rachel Carson's Greater Washington, D.C.

The stories in **Attractions** will inform you, entertain you, surprise you, and perhaps even shock you. At the same time, you will be building your knowledge about the geography of the United States.

The map below shows the locations of the sites featured in each of the four books. Those contained in *It's Colossal* are highlighted in blue.

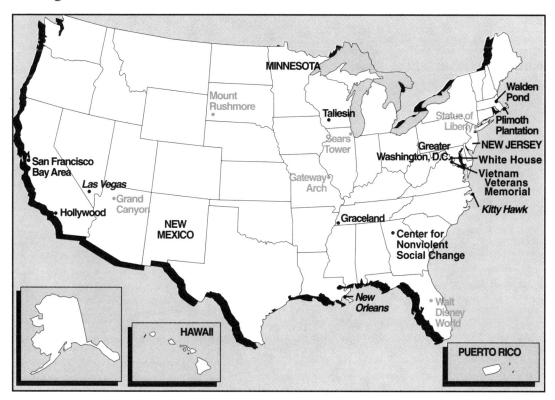

Once you've read the stories in *It's Colossal*, we invite you to explore the other three books in the **Attractions** series. As you do, you'll learn the stories behind some of the most famous places in America.

The Statue of Liberty after its 1986 renovation

GOLDEN DOOR

Is the Statue of Liberty really American?
To find out, read on. . . .

A $70 Million Face-Lift

1   One spring day in 1980, two men chose a strange spot for camping out. They climbed partway up the outside of the Statue of Liberty. Then they spread out their sleeping bags. They ate dinner and spent the night on a fold of Liberty's robe. Next morning, they were fine. But what about the statue?

2   People feared that the climbers' equipment had damaged Liberty. A complete inspection followed. That's how Americans found out that the nation's tallest and most beloved statue was in bad condition. The climbers weren't to blame. The real villains were time, weather, water, and pollution. Liberty needed a face-lift, but her problems were more than skin deep. She needed internal surgery, too. Americans donated generously. Children even broke their banks and sent in their pennies. To restore Liberty, Americans spent $70 million—about 154 times the statue's original cost!

3   Liberty got a complete cleaning, inside and out. The lighting, ventilation, and elevator systems were all improved. Her iron framework and copper "skin" were repaired. Liberty also held a new torch with a flame made of

gold leaf. The light that seems to shine from the torch at night is the reflection of spotlights below. The work was finished in time for her centennial birthday party on July 4, 1986. For a 100-year-old woman, she was in great shape.

4 Every year, more than 2.5 million tourists go to see the Statue of Liberty. They get to Liberty Island by taking a 15-minute ferryboat ride. Some are satisfied to see the statue's exterior and the exhibits in the pedestal. But the more daring want to climb to the top. Visitors can take stairs or an elevator from the pedestal to the base of the statue. From there on, their feet must do the work. It's quite a climb! The interior of the statue has two stairways that wind up to the crown. Visitors must climb 162 steps (about 12 flights) on a narrow, winding stairway. However, there are rest seats at every third turn of the spiral. When they finally get to the top, their efforts are rewarded. From the observation deck in Liberty's crown, about 40 tourists at a time can enjoy a beautiful view of New York Harbor.

Checking Comprehension

How did Americans learn about the condition of the
    Statue of Liberty?
What repairs were made on the Statue of Liberty?
How do visitors get to the top of the statue?

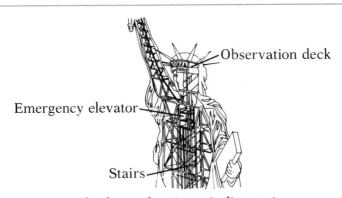

Cross section of Liberty showing winding stairway, emergency elevator, and observation deck

5 In the late 1770s, French military supplies and leadership helped the American colonies win their War of Independence. In 1789, the new American democracy inspired the French Revolution. These two nations share a long friendship and a great love of liberty.

6 One evening in 1865, a French scholar was entertaining friends. He wanted France to give a gift to the American people. Someone suggested a colossal monument. One of the dinner guests that evening was a young sculptor, Frédéric-Auguste Bartholdi [Bar·tall'dee]. He wanted to design this huge sculpture.

7 In 1871, Bartholdi came to the United States to sell the idea to important Americans. Bartholdi's ship sailed into New York Harbor. He decided that this busy harbor was the perfect place for his huge monument. He imagined an enormous woman holding a torch. She would be a symbol of liberty enlightening[1] the world.

8 Bartholdi's interest in the project won many supporters. An agreement was made. The French would pay for and build the statue. The Americans would pay for and build the pedestal.[2] The French raised the $400,000 needed, some of it by holding a huge lottery. Bartholdi went to work. Early in 1885, Lady Liberty was ready for delivery. But there was no pedestal for her in New York Harbor. The Americans were still $100,000 short of their goal, which was an embarrassing situation.

9 Then a New York newspaper publisher found a way to encourage donations. He offered to print the names of all donors in his newspaper. Within a few months, about

---

[1]giving knowledge to
[2]bottom support

121,000 Americans had sent in $101,000. The Americans finally had $270,000 to build the pedestal. The last donation came from the famous inventor Thomas Alva Edison.

10   In 1886, Liberty was placed on her pedestal. She was dedicated at a big celebration. When the big day came, Bartholdi stood inside her head. He was waiting to pull the string that would release the cloth covering. A boy standing hundreds of feet below was supposed to signal him at the right moment. Then President Grover Cleveland arrived and received a 21-gun salute. Bartholdi's signalman got lost in the smoke. The crowd below was made up almost entirely of men. Then a few hundred uninvited women arrived. Their leader insisted on speaking. She liked the idea of a female Liberty. But American women didn't even have the right to vote! No one could miss the irony[3] of that. Suddenly, another cannon boomed. Confused, Bartholdi pulled the cord before the signal. The cover fell off, and the cheering crowd met Liberty Enlightening the World.

Checking Comprehension

Why did the French want to give the United States this gift?

Who paid for the statue and its pedestal?

Why were Americans embarrassed when the statue was completed?

---

[3] the opposite of what is expected

11   From head to foot, Liberty is a series of symbols. The seven spikes of her crown stand for the seven continents and the seven seas. (The term *the seven seas* means all the bodies of water in the world.) Her raised right hand holds the torch of freedom. Her left hand holds a tablet dated July 4, 1776. This is the date the Declaration of Independence was signed. The broken chain around her feet represents the end of tyranny.[4]

12   Everyone admired Liberty's dignity and beauty. But who was the model? Bartholdi refused to tell. The secret died with him. The best guess about Liberty's face is that the model was Bartholdi's mother. In 1884, one of Bartholdi's friends told an audience this story: One evening, Bartholdi invited him to the opera. Sitting in Bartholdi's box was an old woman. When the light fell on her face, the friend said, "Why, she's your model for the Statue of Liberty!" Bartholdi replied, "Yes, it's my mother." Listening to his friend tell this story, Bartholdi's eyes filled with tears. But he never publicly admitted or denied the likeness.

13   The model for the figure is also a mystery. According to one French author, she was a French model. But does this mean that this great symbol of the United States isn't American at all? Well, she is at least a little American. The model for Liberty's foot may have been a Chicago girl that the sculptor met during one of his trips to the States.

Checking Comprehension

What was Liberty originally designed to stand for?
Whose face did Bartholdi's friends believe Liberty was
    modeled after?

---

[4]cruel and unjust government

14   What is Liberty made of? Three hundred thin copper sheets form the "skin" of the statue. These green sheets are attached to each other with rivets. An iron "skeleton" supports the statue. This framework was built by Alexandre-Gustave Eiffel [Eye'ful], the designer of the Eiffel Tower in Paris. He solved the engineering problem of how to support this huge, heavy figure.

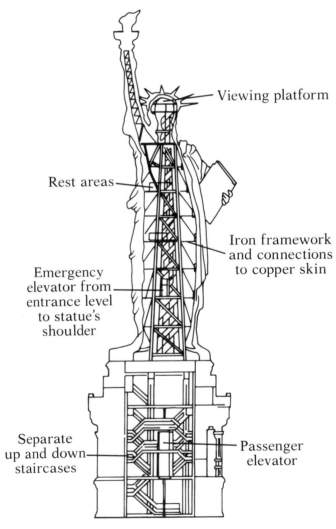

"Skeleton" of Statue of Liberty showing its interior

15   The completed Liberty was displayed in Paris in 1884. At that time, it was the largest statue in the world. From its base to the tip of its torch, it measured more than 151 feet. It weighed about 200 tons! To travel to the United States, it was taken apart and packed in 214 wooden boxes. In New York, the statue was put together again on its pedestal. The 10-story concrete, granite, and steel pedestal building was designed by a famous American architect, Richard Morris Hunt. Statue and pedestal together are 305 feet high!

16   Liberty stands on Liberty Island, about 1.5 miles from the tip of Manhattan. Millions of immigrants passed this small island as they entered the United States by ship. Liberty was waiting there to welcome them, promising freedom and opportunity.

17   The idea of the statue as the "mother of exiles"[5] came from a poem by Emma Lazarus. She was an American writer from a rich family. She gave a great deal of money and organized relief efforts to help immigrants. Lazarus's poem, "The New Colossus,"[6] was written on a tablet inside the pedestal in 1903. In the poem, Liberty speaks to other nations and says, "Give me your tired, your poor, / Your huddled masses yearning to breathe free. . . ." At the end of the poem, Liberty says, "I lift my lamp beside the golden door."

Checking Comprehension

How did Liberty come to the United States?

What has she come to symbolize since 1903?

---

[5]people forced to leave their native countries

[6]a gigantic statue, the original Colossus was a statue of Apollo

Coming to America

18   About a half-mile north of Liberty Island is another American landmark, Ellis Island. For 12 million people, the immigrant experience began here. Ellis Island was the country's first federal immigration facility. About 100 million living Americans (42 percent of the nation's population) have ancestors who passed through Ellis Island.

19   From 1901 to 1917, Ellis Island received 2,000–5,000 people a day! What was it like when they got off the ship? Newcomers speaking dozens of different languages were led into the baggage room. "Check your bags here," the guides told them. But many were afraid to let go of their suitcases and other possessions. They carried everything around with them while they went through inspection. Sometimes that took hours, sometimes days.

20   Exhausted and confused, most immigrants worried about only one thing. Would they be sent back? If they were sick or had a criminal record, deportation[7] was likely. Actually, only about 250,000 (2 percent) of Ellis Island arrivals were deported. Some never made it to the mainland for another reason. Between 1892 and 1932, there were 3,000 suicides on Ellis Island.

21   Two lines of immigrants walked up the high stairway to the Great Hall. Doctors watched as they climbed the stairs. A possible medical problem? They marked the person's clothing with chalk: *H* for heart disease, *E* for eye trouble, and so on. Later, those with chalk marks got more careful medical exams than the others. People who were mentally ill or had trachoma [truh·ko'ma][8] were deported. Some sick people were sent to the Ellis Island hospital.

---

[7]removing an immigrant from the country
[8]a serious, contagious eye disease

22   Frightened immigrants waited in the enormous Great Hall to talk to an immigration official. The interview was usually brief. "What's your name? Your occupation? Where are you going to live? Do you have any relatives here? Do you want to overthrow the government?" Communication was hard. Immigrants' names were sometimes shortened. When the interview ended, the newcomers walked down another stairway. The left aisle was for those going to New York. The right one was for those going to other cities. The unlucky ones were sent down the center aisle. That path led to further inspection, detention,[9] a hearing, or deportation.

Ellis Island's newly restored Main Building in 1990

Checking Comprehension

What kind of inspection did immigrants get?

What percentage of immigrants were deported from Ellis Island?

---

[9]the act of holding a person back

23   From 1924 on, the United States placed strict limits on the numbers of immigrants let in. As the century progressed, a smaller percentage of immigrants entered the United States by way of New York. In 1954, Ellis Island was closed. After that, vandals and bad weather did great damage to the buildings. In the late 1960s and early 1970s, a small section was cleaned up. It was opened to the public in 1976. But the big change occurred in the 1980s. In 1982, the Statue of Liberty–Ellis Island Foundation was set up. It raised $230 million to restore both facilities. About $160 million was spent to fix up Ellis Island.

24   Ellis Island's main building is now a museum. Visitors can see a beautifully restored Great Hall. Some exhibits feature old photographs or "treasures" that immigrants brought from the old country. Audiotapes bring immigrants' memories to the listener. Some displays can be operated by visitors. Some involve computers. Two theaters show the prize-winning movie *Island of Hope, Island of Tears*.

25   Outside is the American Immigrant Wall of Honor. It has more than 400,000 names on it. Relatives donated $100 for each listing.

26   Since the nation's beginnings, about 60 million people have come to the United States to live. This was the largest human migration in modern history. Ellis Island honors their courage, suffering, and hope.

Checking Comprehension

Why do immigrants no longer arrive at Ellis Island?
What is Ellis Island used for today?

SIDELIGHTS
About the Statue of Liberty

The Statue of Liberty is no small lady.
- Her head measures 17.3 feet from the top of the skull to the chin.
- Each eye is 2.5 feet wide.
- Her nose is 4.5 feet long.
- Her right arm is 42 feet long and 12 feet wide at its widest point.

Is she the tallest statue in the world? Not anymore. Now that title belongs to a Russian sculpture built in 1967. This female figure, *Motherland*, measures 270 feet!

Liberty's Twin

The Statue of Liberty has a smaller twin sister across the ocean. In 1885, some Americans living in Paris wanted to say *merci* to the French. What was the perfect gift? Of course, a Statue of Liberty. The French version, about one-fourth the size of the American statue, stands on an island in the Seine River.

About New York City (the Big Apple)

In 1626, Dutch settlers bought the island of Manhattan from local Native Americans for the equivalent of $24. Today, Manhattan is part of New York City, the largest American city, with a population of more than seven million. New York City has five boroughs: Manhattan, the Bronx, Queens, Brooklyn, and Staten Island. Four of these political divisions are on islands.

Making Inferences

Reread the paragraph(s) indicated after each statement.
Then decide if each statement is probably true or false.

_____ 1. Liberty is very heavy because her inside is solid.
     (paragraph 4)
_____ 2. The Statue of Liberty was made in France.
     (paragraphs 6, 8)
_____ 3. Americans of the 1980s and 1990s were more
     enthusiastic about the Statue of Liberty than
     Americans of the early 1880s were. (paragraphs
     2, 8–9)
_____ 4. In the 1880s, American women were treated as
     the equals of men. (paragraph 10)
_____ 5. When new immigrants saw the Statue of Liberty,
     they felt safe. (paragraph 16)
_____ 6. Most of today's Ellis Island visitors once landed
     there as new immigrants. (paragraph 18)

Practicing Vocabulary

Part A. Circle the words that mean very big.

colossal	**enormous**	**gigantic**
embarrassing	**exhausting**	**huge**

Part B. Choose the correct words to complete each
sentence.

1. The Statue of Liberty stands on a stone (pedestal,
   torch, symbol, island) in New York Harbor.
2. It must be very (embarrassing, exhausting, easy,
   enthusiastic) to climb up the stairs to Liberty's crown.
3. In her right hand, Liberty holds a (tablet, torch,
   pedestal, ton).

4. It cost millions of dollars to (build, restore, transport, donate) the Statue of Liberty.
5. The Statue of Liberty is one of the most (embarrassing, favorite, popular, large) statues in the world.

Talking It Over

1. An 1885 newspaper cartoon showed Uncle Sam in front of the Statue of Liberty, holding his hat out. What did it mean?
2. The American people helped raise money for the Statue of Liberty's pedestal and, later, for the restoration of Ellis Island. Tell how.
3. Why do you think Bartholdi refused to tell who modeled for the Statue of Liberty?
4. Do you think the nation's symbol of liberty should be a woman? Why or why not?
5. If the United States built a symbol of liberty now, what do you think it would look like?
6. Why do you think New York City is called the Big Apple?

Sears Tower dominating the skyline in downtown Chicago

SKY HIGH

*Sears Tower looks very big, doesn't it? In fact, it's big
enough to hold the universe inside. Sound impossible?
Read on. . . .*

Reaching the Top—
the Hard Way

1   It was Memorial Day, May 25, 1981, at 3:00 A.M. Downtown
Chicago was dark and quiet. No one saw the strange-look-
ing young man in the red and blue costume standing beside
the world's tallest building. Daniel Goodwin, then 25 years
old, was dressed from head to toe in his $450 Spider-Man
outfit. Unlike the comic strip character, "Spider Dan"
wasn't chasing a criminal. He wanted to climb Sears Tower
just for the challenge.

2   Helped by a friend with a ladder, Dan began climbing.
Dan Goodwin wasn't crazy. He wasn't trying to kill himself. He was an experienced mountain climber and acro-
bat.[1] Before he began his climb, he studied the building for
weeks and planned his route. Spider Dan used suction cups
and a claw-shaped tool to cling to the side of the building.
He climbed along the tracks for the automatic window
washers.

---

[1]a gymnast who can do difficult physical movements

3   By 6:10 A.M., Dan was at the 16th floor. Then some Sears Tower workers saw him. At 6:45, firefighters arrived and tried to talk Dan into giving up. But Spider Dan wouldn't quit. He just kept climbing higher and higher. About 7:40, the firefighters climbed onto a platform and tried to reach him. He moved sideways to avoid them. At 8:45, he was at the 50th floor. By then, news of his climb had been on radio and TV. A crowd of spectators[2] stood on the sidewalk below.

"Spider Dan" Goodwin climbing Sears Tower with high-rise buildings in background

4   The firefighters decided to compromise[3] with Dan. They agreed to let him keep climbing if he tied a rope around his waist. As the climb continued, more people arrived to watch. They came in cars and taxicabs, on foot,

_____

[2]people watching an event
[3]to form an agreement in which each side partially gives in to the wishes of the other side

on bicycles—even on roller skates. As Dan approached the roof, he tried to put up an American flag, but it was too windy.

5   At 10:25 A.M.—about 7½ hours after he started—Dan Goodwin reached the roof of Sears Tower, at the 110th floor, 1,454 feet (443 meters) up in the sky. He had climbed the world's tallest building! What was Dan's reward for his amazing accomplishment? The police were waiting for him at the top of the Tower. They arrested him for trespassing[4] on private property.

6   Two years later, Goodwin climbed New York City's World Trade Center, the second tallest building in the world. Once again, crowds cheered when he reached the top, 1,350 feet above the ground. Once again, Spider Dan was arrested—this time for giving an illegal street demonstration.

Checking Comprehension

Why did Dan Goodwin want to climb Sears Tower?
Why did the firefighters want to stop him?
What compromise did Dan and the firefighters make?

Amazing Facts About the Sears Tower

7   Spider Dan took the slow way up. Most Sears Tower visitors take a faster, safer, indoor route. They ascend[5] the world's tallest building by high-speed elevator. During the climb, the talking elevator boasts about its great speed. It has a right to brag. Riders zip from the lower level to the 103rd floor skydeck in about one minute!

8   From there, they can look out in all four directions. They see the nation's third largest city spread out around

---

[4]going on someone's property without permission
[5]go up

them. A recorded voice points out the sights. They include Lake Michigan, the Chicago River, and the city's many famous buildings and museums. On a clear day, visitors can see out for 50 miles. The view takes in parts of Indiana, Wisconsin, and Michigan. On a summer night, Chicago's famous Buckingham Fountain puts on a show. It glows with colored lights as it shoots water 90 feet high.

9   Sears Tower is not only the world's tallest building. It is also the world's largest private office building, with 4.5 million square feet of space. Only the Pentagon (home of the U.S. Defense Department) is larger. Sears Tower may look slender, but it is actually quite a heavyweight. At 225,500 tons, it would break any scale it stood on.

10   When construction began in 1970, Sears, Roebuck and Co. was the world's largest retailer. The company chairman felt Sears should have the world's largest headquarters. From 1973 until 1992, Sears housed about 6,500 employees there. Then Sears moved most of its national headquarters to a Chicago suburb. The company still owns the Tower. But it doesn't occupy much of it anymore.

11   Other businesses moved into the offices. At least 20,000 people go in and out of Sears Tower each day. This figure includes those who work there full-time, those who stop in for business purposes, and tourists. To serve them, Sears Tower has 7 restaurants and 30 shops.

12   How do so many people get around in this huge space? The Tower's 104-car elevator system includes 14 express elevators. They go nonstop to "skylobbies" on the 33rd and 34th floors and the 66th and 67th floors. From there, passengers transfer to local elevators to reach higher floors. There are also 18 escalators[6] in the building.

---

[6]moving stairways

13   Sears Tower also has an amazing work of art, an enormous sculpture in motion. Alexander Calder's *Universe* is in a glassed-in lobby 56 feet high. Calder, an American artist, was famous for his mobiles. Many of his works move when air blows on them. This one has seven motors. Each moves a different part of *Universe* at a different speed. The sculpture includes three flowers, a spine, a spiral tube, a sun, and a pendulum.[7] *Universe* is 55 feet long and 33 feet high and weighs 16,000 pounds. It's a fascinating study in color and movement.

Alexander Calder's Universe *sculpture*

Checking Comprehension

How do people get to the 42nd floor of Sears Tower?
How does the Tower hold the universe inside it?

---

[7]a structure that hangs and swings freely in the air

14   Architects from Skidmore, Owings and Merrill began work on Sears Tower in 1970. Designing a structure this tall was a challenge. The taller a building is, the more trouble it has with its worst enemy, the wind. A world-famous building engineer named Fazlur Khan [Konn] and his partners designed the Tower to be wind-resistant. On its lower levels, Sears Tower is supported by nine square steel tubes in three connected rows of three. As the building gets higher, the number of tubes decreases. This stepback design is both attractive and practical. Even in Chicago's strongest winds, the building sways no more than six inches.

15   Visitors to the Tower don't have to worry about fire or about getting trapped in the building. Sears Tower has one of the most complete safety systems ever designed for a high rise. Its steel is fireproof. Automatic water sprinklers and smoke detectors are on every floor. If a power failure occurs, two diesel generators will provide backup power for elevators and lighting. The building also has fire pumping stations, a public address system,[8] and hot lines[9] to the fire and police departments.

16   Lightning is no threat to Sears Tower, either. Every year, the building is struck by lightning about one thousand times. But no damage or injury results.

Checking Comprehension

What safety features protect Sears Tower from fire?
What design features allow it to stand up to strong
    winds?

---

[8]loudspeakers placed so that announcements can be heard
  throughout the building
[9]telephones connected directly with the police and fire
  departments

A Short History of Skyscrapers

17   The tallest skyscrapers are in Chicago and New York, but many other American cities also have some. For example, there are skyscrapers in Los Angeles, Houston, Dallas, and Seattle. Of the 21 tallest buildings in the world, some are outside the United States, in Hong Kong, Singapore, and Toronto.

18   How tall is a skyscraper? There's no exact answer. Of the 21 tallest, the number of floors ranges from 46 to 110. The height range is from 875 feet to 1,454 feet (from 267 meters to 443 meters). Today, the word *skyscraper* is used for a very tall building with a steel structure.

19   Chicago was the birthplace of the skyscraper. Strangely enough, this was because of a cow. One windy evening in 1871, a Chicagoan named Mrs. Patrick O'Leary was milking her cow in her barn. The cow kicked over the lighted lantern. The hay caught fire, and the wind blew the flames toward the rest of the city. The fire raged for 3½ days. Mrs. O'Leary and her cow survived, but 1,500 buildings did not. That was about one-third of the city. The disaster is known as the Great Chicago Fire.

20   Before the fire, the tallest buildings in Chicago were only six stories high. Many built soon after the fire were no taller. Then several famous architects came to Chicago. They were drawn by the chance to rebuild a great city. Their arrival changed everything.

21   In the 1880s, engineers and architects found that they could build much taller buildings than before for two reasons. First, hydraulic[10] and electric elevators became available. Second, strong, lightweight steel frames could be built for support. The idea of building up rather than out was appealing. Land was expensive in downtown Chicago. The

---

[10]operated by water or oil pressure

city's first skyscraper was a 10-story building built in 1883. In 1891, Chicago's 20-story Masonic Temple became the tallest building in the world.

22   Today, Chicago is home to some of the world's tallest skyscrapers. The Amoco Building, Chicago's second tallest building, has 80 stories and is 1,136 feet tall. The John Hancock Center, 1,127 feet high, has 100 stories. It's also the tallest Chicago skyscraper that is used for many purposes. "Big John" is both an office building and an apartment building.

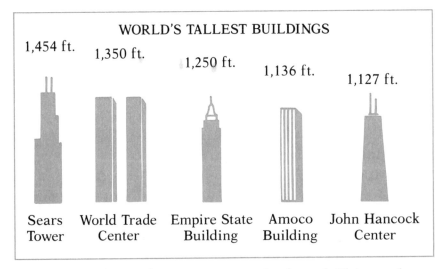

WORLD'S TALLEST BUILDINGS

1,454 ft.   1,350 ft.   1,250 ft.   1,136 ft.   1,127 ft.

Sears Tower   World Trade Center   Empire State Building   Amoco Building   John Hancock Center

23   During the 20th century, New York and Chicago have taken turns being the home of the tallest skyscraper. Where will it all end? In the 1950s, the great American architect Frank Lloyd Wright drew designs for a mile-high (5,280 feet) skyscraper. It was to have 528 floors. Who knows what the technology and the dreamers of the future will create? The sky is the limit.

Checking Comprehension
How did a cow affect Chicago architecture?
Why does a skyscraper need steel?

SIDELIGHTS

About Sears Tower

What's Sears Tower made of?
- a 76,000-ton steel framework
- enough concrete to build an eight-lane highway 5 miles long
- a 28-acre aluminum "skin"
- 16,000 bronze-tinted windows
- 145,000 light fixtures
- 1,500 miles of electrical wiring
- enough telephone wiring to wrap around the earth 1¾ times!

About Chicago

What's in a name?

Everyone agrees that the name *Chicago* comes from an American Indian word. But what does it mean? Some say it's an Indian word for powerful. Others say that it means skunk or onion. It's said that onions once grew along the Chicago River and gave the area a strong, unpleasant smell. In other words, to its Native American residents a few hundred years ago, Chicago may have been Stinkytown.

Why is Chicago called the Windy City? It may be because of the strong winds from Lake Michigan. But, more likely, the name was inspired by 19th-century politicians. They boasted a lot. Some people thought they were windy, or full of hot air.

Making Inferences

Reread the paragraph(s) indicated after each statement.
Then decide if each statement is probably true or false.

_____ 1. Goodwin began his climb when it was still dark out because he wanted to reach the top before anyone saw him. (paragraph 1)

_____ 2. The firefighters' biggest worry was that Goodwin would damage the building. (paragraphs 3–4)

_____ 3. A meter is longer than a foot. (paragraph 5)

_____ 4. It took about three years to build Sears Tower. (paragraph 10)

_____ 5. Sears Tower doesn't have apartments for rent. (paragraphs 9, 22)

Practicing Vocabulary

Choose six of the following nine words to complete the sentences.

boast	**high-rise**	**skyline**
challenge	**sidewalk**	**skyscrapers**
elevator	**sight-seers**	**spectators**

1. Chicago residents have many famous and beautiful

   buildings to _____ about.

2. One of Chicago's most famous _____ is the

   100-story John Hancock Center.

3. Many _____ go to the observatory at the top

   of "Big John."

4. To get there, they take the fastest _____ in the world. They travel from the ground floor to the top in 39 seconds.

5. From Chicago's Outer Drive, along the lake, visitors enjoy a good view of the city's _____, the outline of the skyscrapers and other _____ buildings against the sky.

Talking It Over

1. Define and compare a skyscraper and a high rise. Is every skyscraper a high rise? Is every high rise a skyscraper?
2. What's the tallest building in your hometown? Is it a skyscraper? What is it used for?
3. Would you like to live in a high-rise building or a skyscraper? What are some advantages? What are some disadvantages?
4. What kind of person is Dan Goodwin? Make a list of words that describe him.
5. Would you like to do something dangerous or unusual? What would you like to do? Why?
6. Tell about a time when you faced a challenge or made a compromise.

The Gateway Arch rising from the west bank of the Mississippi River

GATEWAY
TO THE WEST

Look carefully at the Gateway Arch. Compare its height to its width at its base. Is it taller than it is wide or vice versa? To find out, read on. . . .

Arch of Triumph

1   In 1947, the city of St. Louis held a contest to select a design for an important memorial. It would honor the people who settled the American West and the president who made it all possible—Thomas Jefferson. First prize was $40,000. The contest attracted 172 entries.

2   Among them were separate entries from a father and a son, partners in a Michigan architectural firm. The family had come to America from Finland in 1923. Eliel Saarinen [Sah'ri·nen] was a famous architect. His son, 37-year-old Eero, wasn't well-known.

3   The contest judges didn't know the names of the designers. Each entry was identified only by number. The judges chose five finalists. But they already knew that their favorite was entry number 144, the magnificent soaring arch. Eliel Saarinen received a telegram congratulating him. For three days, everyone at Saarinen's office cele-

brated his achievement. Then another telegram arrived. It offered apologies to the father and congratulations to the correct winner, his son Eero.

4   Eero's design used the latest in 20th-century know-how. Nothing like it had ever been built before. Like the pioneers he honored, Saarinen bravely tried the untried. His choice of an arch also seemed just right. An arch encloses space, but it also leaves it open. So did westward expansion.

5   Saarinen's prize-winning arch looked perfect on paper. But no one knew how to build it. Luckily, construction was delayed because of a lack of funds. As far back as the 1930s, the U.S. government had promised to supply most of the money needed to build a memorial. But the expenses of various wars stood in the way. The delays gave engineers several years to help Saarinen. Together, they designed a structure that could stand firmly on its own two legs.

6   In 1957, the government finally came up with $3 million. St. Louis provided another $1 million. Groundbreaking took place in 1959. Then, in 1961, Eero Saarinen died of a brain tumor. He never saw the arch he had spent so many years designing. But, by the time of his death, he was famous throughout the world for many other architectural works. The building of the Gateway Arch began in 1962. It was completed in 1965 and cost about $13 million. Many features of the total memorial were added after that, including one of the largest museums in the national park system.

Checking Comprehension

Who and what does the Gateway Arch honor?
What delayed construction of the Gateway Arch?
Why is the Gateway Arch as much a memorial to
     Saarinen as it was to Jefferson?

---

7 No one can visit St. Louis and not see the Gateway Arch. It stands on the west bank of the Mississippi River, reaching 630 feet into the sky. This slender giant towers over the city skyline. A statue twice as tall as Liberty and her pedestal could easily fit under it. Of course, the Eiffel Tower in Paris (984 feet high) is much taller. So are many American skyscrapers. Still, the majestic Gateway Arch is the tallest arch in the world and is our country's tallest monument.

8 Its appearance is deceiving.[1] It looks slim and fragile. But it actually weighs 43,000 tons! Its shape fools the eye, too. It looks taller than it is wide. But its height and its width at the bottom are exactly the same. Why does it trick the eye that way? The Gateway Arch becomes narrower as it goes up. That makes it appear taller than it really is.

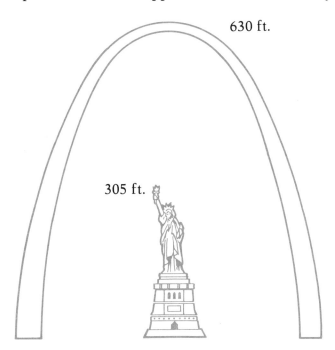

Liberty's height compared to the height of the Gateway Arch

---

[1] likely to confuse or mislead

9   How safe is it? Very. It is supported by foundations that go deep into the ground. Its curve is the most stable[2] shape possible for a standing arch. The tapered legs make the structure more wind-resistant.

10   The structure of the Gateway Arch is like a sandwich. The outside is polished stainless steel. The inner frame is structural steel. Between the steel layers is concrete, going up 300 feet. Buried in the concrete are 252 steel rods in each leg of the Arch. They go deep into the underground foundation.

11   What if the wind huffs and puffs? Can it blow the Gateway Arch down? Not likely. The Arch was designed to withstand earthquakes and 150-mile-per-hour winds. It can safely sway up to 18 inches at the top. But it usually moves no more than an inch.

12   Traveling to the top is an adventure. The journey begins 50 feet below ground. An eight-car tram gives tourists a four-minute ride up the inside of a curved leg. The cars stay level by rotating horizontally as they climb. Near the top, passengers get out. They walk up a short flight of stairs to the observation room. There, they enjoy a 30-mile view.

Checking Comprehension

What does the Gateway Arch look like?

Do visitors ride up its inside or its outside?

---

[2]not easy to move or break apart

13   Many visitors go from the heights to the depths. After visiting the top of the Arch, they visit the Museum of Westward Expansion. It's hidden underground, between the Arch's legs. The Gateway Arch and the Museum of Westward Expansion are really one memorial. It's called the Jefferson National Expansion Memorial.

14   The museum's exhibits show the people, animals, and artifacts of the Old West. Colorful murals of the West deck the walls. Mounted animals stand about—the beaver, the grizzly bear, the bison,[3] and the Indian pony. There's an Indian tepee made of buffalo skin and an original Oregon Trail wagon. A theater shows a film about the building of the Arch. A sculpture of Thomas Jefferson watches over all.

Statue of President Thomas Jefferson in the Museum of Westward Expansion

Checking Comprehension

Why can't visitors see the Museum of Westward Expansion when they are standing near the Gateway Arch?

What does the museum contain?

---

[3]commonly called the American buffalo

A $15 Million Bargain

15   In 1800, the United States stretched from the Atlantic Ocean west to the Mississippi River. The land west of the Mississippi was owned by other countries. Native Americans lived there. Most Americans didn't even know what the West looked like. Then, in 1801, Thomas Jefferson became the nation's third president. Westward expansion was on its way.

16   In 1800, France made a secret treaty with Spain that gave France a very large piece of land in North America. It was the Louisiana Territory, and it covered about 828,000 square miles. It went west from the Mississippi River to the Rocky Mountains. It stretched south from Canada to the Gulf of Mexico. Napoleon, then emperor of France, needed money to finance a war with England. So he offered to sell this huge territory to the United States. The price? A mere $15 million.

17   President Jefferson wanted to take Napoleon's offer. But was it legal? The Constitution didn't give the government power to buy new land. But it did permit a president to make treaties (if the Senate approved). Jefferson decided that he could make a treaty to buy land. Jefferson knew that he was stretching the Constitution. The senators knew it, too. But the price was cheap, and they wanted the land. So, in 1803, the treaty was signed. At that moment, the United States doubled in size. The Louisiana Territory later became all or part of 15 states.

Checking Comprehension

Who sold the Louisiana Territory to the United States?
How did Jefferson stretch the Constitution?

---

18 What was in this huge, unknown territory? And what was the best way to cross it? Jefferson decided to find out. In 1804, he asked two men to lead a group of explorers through the Louisiana Territory. They were Meriwether Lewis and William Clark.

19 With 51 others, Lewis and Clark left St. Louis in 1804. Their travels took them far west of the Louisiana Territory. They went all the way to the Pacific Ocean. As they traveled, friendly Indians gave them food, shelter, transportation, and guidance. The explorers learned a lot about the waterways and the natural wealth of the West.

20 Lewis and Clark discovered many strange plants and wild animals. Some of them American scientists knew little or nothing about. One of these was the grizzly bear, weighing 800 pounds and standing eight feet tall! Other discoveries were the prairie dog, the American antelope, and the mountain goat. The explorers wrote good descriptions of what they found. They also brought back samples.

21 They were gone for two years. People back in St. Louis thought they were dead. The expedition traveled by boat, canoe, and horseback. Round-trip, they covered more than 8,000 miles. When they returned to St. Louis, their reports were glowing. Their stories sparked widespread interest in heading West.

Checking Comprehension

When did the Lewis and Clark expedition return?
What did it accomplish?

---

22   By 1848, the territory of the United States had grown far beyond the Louisiana Territory. In 1846, England and the United States agreed to divide the Oregon Territory in half. The upper part became British Columbia. The lower half eventually became the states of Washington, Oregon, and Idaho, and parts of Montana and Wyoming.

23   As a result of the Mexican War, the United States got another 525,000 square miles of land in 1848. It included present-day California, Nevada, and Utah, most of Arizona and New Mexico, and parts of Colorado and Wyoming. Twelve years earlier, in 1836, Texas declared its independence from Mexico. Nine years later, it became a state. With these additions, the country stretched from the Atlantic to the Pacific, as shown in the map below.

24   The city of St. Louis became the gateway to the new territories. Its location was perfect. Here, the nation's two longest rivers meet. The Missouri River cuts through the

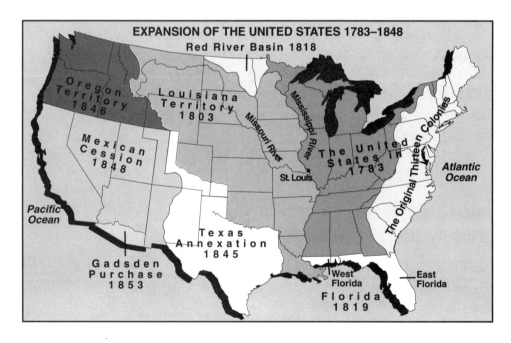

state going east and west. The Mississippi runs north and south. St. Louis quickly became an important trade and transportation center.

25 Among the earliest explorers of the West were hunters called mountain men. They lived alone in the mountains all year, hunting and trapping. Fur trading was a good business until about 1840. Then overhunting made beavers scarce. Also, fur hats went out of style. The era of the mountain men ended.

26 Next came the pioneers. Between 1841 and 1861, about 300,000 pioneers made the overland journey west. Families traveled in covered wagons pulled by oxen. They took all their possessions with them. Many wagon trains started from Missouri. Their guides were men who knew the West well. Sometimes they were on the trail for months. They fought bad weather, flooding, drought, food shortages, and disease. Hostile Indians killed only a few hundred of them. More often, pioneers killed or injured themselves by mishandling their guns. About 5 percent died on the journey.

27 Two big attractions spurred westward expansion. One was the discovery of gold in California in 1848. The second was inexpensive and, later, free land. In the mid-19th century, Western land could be bought dirt cheap. The price? Just $1.25 an acre! Then, in 1862, the Homestead Act provided that any adult head of a household could get 160 acres free. In return, the family had to live on the land for five years and improve it. The Homestead Act brought another 500,000 families to the West.

Checking Comprehension

Why did St. Louis become the gateway to the West?
Why were pioneers attracted to the West?
Why was traveling West difficult and risky?

The Last Frontier

28   After the Civil War ended in 1865, the Great Plains began to fill up with ranchers and cowboys. For some years, cattle roamed freely until roundup time. Then they were taken to the nearest railroad and sent to market. The farmers began to complain about animals eating their crops. In 1872, barbed wire was invented. It put an end to the open range.

29   By 1890, the United States had developed the land all the way to the Pacific Ocean. There was no longer a Western frontier. Railroads crossed the country. Native Americans lived on reservations. Bison, which had once roamed the plains in great herds, were almost extinct. Westward expansion had changed the Wild West.

30   Of course, progress isn't a one-way street. The development of the West also destroyed much. Many Indian cultures were lost. Plants, animals, and the landscape were all affected. Railroads brought pollution along with transportation. Did Americans tame the West or destroy it? People will argue both sides. But right or wrong, it took courage to turn wilderness into towns and cities.

31   "Go west, young man," was popular advice in the 19th century. Hunters, pioneers, miners, railroad workers, farmers, and others took the challenge. The Jefferson National Expansion Memorial remembers and honors them all.

Checking Comprehension

What attracted people to the Great Plains?
In what ways did progress destroy the West?

SIDELIGHTS

About the Gateway Arch

- The legs of the Gateway Arch are triangles. At ground level, they are 54 feet on each side. At the top, they are 17 feet on each side.
- Saarinen's Arch is as tall as a 63-story building.
- The Arch stands where the village of St. Louis was founded in 1764.
- About 2.5 million tourists visit the Gateway Arch each year.

St. Louis and the Arch

The building of the Gateway Arch led to a rebirth of the city's downtown. Today, tourists can enjoy nice hotels and restaurants, riverboat cruises, a shopping mall, and a sports arena in and near the waterfront.

About Missouri, the Show Me State

The state's earliest residents were ancient Native American mound builders. Their earthen structures can still be seen around the state. The famous writer Mark Twain grew up in Hannibal, Missouri. Visitors tour his childhood home. They also hike through the scary cave described in his novel *Tom Sawyer*. Independence, Missouri, was the home of President Harry Truman. Now, it houses his library, which has 3.5 million items related to his presidency.

According to state lore, Missouri folk can't be tricked by fancy talk. That's why Missouri is called the Show Me State.

Making Inferences

Reread the paragraph(s) indicated after each statement. Then decide if each statement is probably true or false.

_____ 1. Saarinen was a better designer than engineer. (paragraph 5)

_____ 2. Thomas Jefferson did something illegal when he bought the Louisiana Territory. (paragraph 17)

_____ 3. Lewis and Clark went to the West in hopes of getting rich. (paragraph 18)

_____ 4. The West was developed mostly by rich Easterners who bought up Western land. (paragraphs 25–27)

_____ 5. In the 1840s and 1850s, the Far West appealed to settlers more than the Great Plains did. (paragraphs 27–28)

Practicing Vocabulary

Part A. Choose the correct word or phrase to complete each sentence.

1. Eero Saarinen was an (explorer, engineer, architect, emperor).
2. Because Saarinen designed something totally new, he was called (a hero, an architect, an engineer, a pioneer).
3. Lewis and Clark were (mountain men, guides, Native Americans, explorers).
4. In the mid-19th century, families that went to the West to live were called (explorers, pioneers, hunters, designers).
5. The men who led the wagon trains to the Far West were (Native Americans, guides, miners, cowboys).

6. When gold was discovered in California, many people became (hunters, miners, minors, explorers).
7. The employees on the ranches of the Great Plains were called (bison, miners, tourists, cowboys).

Part B. Match each animal with the appropriate description.

1. grizzly bear ——— ridden by cowboys
2. beaver ——— hunted for their fur
3. bison ——— pulled a covered wagon
4. horse ——— roamed the plains
5. ox ——— described by Lewis and Clark

Talking It Over

1. Besides the Gateway Arch, what other famous arches do you know about?
2. In the United States, people are very interested in new ways to do things. They also like to explore new places. Where do we see this pioneering spirit in the United States today?
3. Would you like to have been a pioneer going to the West in 1850? Why or why not?
4. What happened to the Native Americans pushed aside by westward expansion? Where and how do they live now?
5. Do you think American movies have given people a true picture of the West? Why or why not?

Mt. Rushmore's famous faces (left to right): Presidents George Washington, Thomas Jefferson, Theodore Roosevelt, and Abraham Lincoln

HEADS OF STATE

Imagine a person with a Rushmore-sized head.
How tall would he be? Imagine a building as tall as a
Rushmore head. How many floors would it have?
To find out, read on. . . .

Four Granite Faces

1   In 1885, New York lawyer Charles E. Rushmore came to the
Black Hills of South Dakota to do legal work for some
prospectors.[1] The Black Hills were rich with gold and tin.
One spring morning, the group was exploring the scenic
area. The likable young lawyer pointed to one high, rugged
mountain peak. He asked its name. "Never had one," one of
the men said. "But hereafter we'll call 'er Rushmore, by
jingo." And they did.

2   Many years later, American sculptor Gutzon [Goot'son]
Borglum chose Mount Rushmore as the site for his "shrine
of democracy." Charles Rushmore was asked for a donation. He promptly sent a check for $5,000. Today, the name
Rushmore is linked with the names of Washington, Jefferson, Roosevelt, and Lincoln, whose faces are carved there.

---

[1]people searching for valuable minerals in the earth

3   The four presidents on Mount Rushmore represent our nation's greatest ideas and accomplishments during its first 150 years. George Washington led the army during the Revolutionary War. Later, he became the new nation's first president. He symbolizes independence and the birth of the Republic. Thomas Jefferson wrote the Declaration of Independence. He was also our third president. He stands for representative government and westward expansion. Abraham Lincoln, the 16th president, served the nation during the Civil War, when the Southern states left the Union. The North's victory resulted in the reunion of the states and the end of slavery. Lincoln represents the permanent union of our 50 states and the equality of U.S. citizens. Theodore Roosevelt, the first 20th-century president, was responsible for the protection of the nation's forests. He was also responsible for the building of the Panama Canal. This canal allowed American ships to move quickly and easily from the Atlantic Ocean to the Pacific Ocean. It gave the United States international influence.

Checking Comprehension

How did Mount Rushmore get its name?

Where is Mount Rushmore?

What does each president carved on Mount Rushmore represent?

Carving Mount Rushmore

4   The Mount Rushmore National Memorial began with one man's idea. In 1923, South Dakota's state historian, Doane Robinson, wanted to bring more tourists to his state. His idea was to carve huge statues of Western heroes into the Black Hills. In 1924, Robinson invited Borglum to the Black Hills to study his plan. Borglum was an experienced moun-

tain carver. He had worked on the monument to Confederate heroes at Stone Mountain in Georgia.

5   Borglum wanted to do a huge rock sculpture. But he didn't want regional heroes to be the models. He preferred subjects of national importance. He suggested sculptures of Washington and Lincoln. The plan grew from two presidents to three. The men had to look for a bigger mountain than Robinson's first choice.

6   Borglum began by studying the shape of the mountain. Then he designed a grouping of three presidents to fit that shape. (Roosevelt was added later.) Workers found deep cracks in certain sections of the mountain. Borglum's designs had to be changed nine times.

7   Borglum hired miners to recast his models as 60-foot granite heads. At first, these miners knew nothing about sculpture. But they soon became very skilled. First, they marked reference points on the mountain. Then they used

The faces of Presidents George Washington and Thomas Jefferson under construction

dynamite to remove about 450,000 tons of rock. Next, they used pneumatic [new·mat'ic][2] drills to get rid of more granite. When the carving came within three inches of the finished surface, workers drilled small holes close together. Then they chipped off the excess rock. Finally, they smoothed the surfaces with air hammers.

---

[2]operated by compressed air

8   As the men worked, they sat in swinging seats attached to ropes. Borglum watched from below with binoculars. Sometimes he rode up to the site in a small wooden cable car. Then he used a big paint brush to write measurements on the rock. The building of the monument was an engineering feat[3] accomplished by a group. But it was one man's artistic vision. Borglum once said, "I'm making Roosevelt's glasses out of the most precious thing on Earth: imagination."

9   Work on the monument began in 1927. Two years later, the project ran out of money from private donations. The U.S. government agreed to finance it. Often, work stopped while everyone waited for more money, better weather, or both. Borglum worked on the project off and on until his death in 1941. Then his son Lincoln took over. The federal government paid $836,000 of the $990,000 spent on the memorial. Funds ran out again later that year. Gutzon Borglum had wanted to carve the statues to the waist. But, since 1941, no further carving has been done, and none is planned.

Checking Comprehension

Why did it take 14 years to carve the heads?
Are the Mount Rushmore presidents exactly like
    Borglum's models?

---

[3]an accomplishment requiring great skill or talent

A Lasting Impression

10   More than two million tourists visit Mount Rushmore each year. The site is especially popular from Memorial Day to Labor Day. During this period, the sculptor's studio is open. Visitors can see Borglum's models and some of his mountain-carving tools. At night, there's a show in the outdoor theater. The gigantic heads—as tall as a five-story building—are lit up against the black sky. The effect is breathtaking.

11   "How long will it last?" some visitors ask. Granite is a very hard rock. But nothing lasts forever. The heads are wearing away at the rate of one inch every 5,000 years. To prevent damage, repairs are made regularly. Cracks are closed up before water can get inside and freeze. In 1990, geologists studied the monument to see how it was holding up. All four of the famous presidents are aging well. Lincoln's face has a crack across its 20-foot nose. Roosevelt's face has a crack in its forehead. But, in general, the monument is stable.

Checking Comprehension

What can summer visitors see at Mount Rushmore?
Are the heads wearing away quickly or slowly?

Crazy Horse Rides Again

12   Did everyone love Mount Rushmore? Absolutely not. Women's groups complained because there was no woman up there. Nature lovers complained that carving sculpture into a mountain destroyed its natural beauty. But the strongest complaint came from Native American groups. They were angry about this monument honoring U.S. presidents. After all, it was on land taken from their people. To honor Native Americans, another monument is being carved 17 miles from Mount Rushmore. It will be 10 times taller than the Mount Rushmore sculpture! It has its own story to tell.

13   Before European settlers came, Native American tribes—including the Sioux [Sue]—lived in the Black Hills of South Dakota and Wyoming. The Black Hills are not really hills. They are mountain ranges (about 2,000 feet to 7,700 feet high). They aren't really black, either. But dark pine trees on the slopes made the mountains look black from the plains below. So the Sioux called them *paha sapa*

The fifth granite face in the Black Hills of South Dakota emerging. When completed, the mountain carving will look like Sculptor Korczak Ziolkowski's large scale model of Crazy Horse.

(literally, "hills black"). The Sioux also gave South Dakota its name. *Dakota* is the Sioux word for friend or ally.

14   The U.S. government was not a friend to the Sioux. In 1868, it made a treaty with the tribe, establishing the Great Sioux Reservation. This land included a large area in parts of present-day South Dakota, Wyoming, and Montana. Then, in 1874, valuable gold deposits were found in the Black Hills. Thousands of white settlers rushed there. An Indian war chief named Crazy Horse tried to keep the white settlers off Sioux land. In June of 1876, he and other war chiefs won a great victory at the Battle of Little Bighorn. But, by late 1876, many Sioux realized that they were no match for the U.S. Army. Some of them signed a new treaty with the government. They sold their rights to the Black Hills and agreed to live on reservations.

15   In 1877, Crazy Horse and his 1,000 followers came to Fort Robinson, Nebraska, to accept a truce. When the soldiers tried to force him into a jail cell, Crazy Horse resisted. One of the soldiers stabbed Crazy Horse. The great Sioux chief, about 34 years old, died a few hours later. But stories of his great leadership live on.

Checking Comprehension

How did the Black Hills get their name?
Why did the Sioux lose their land?
How was Crazy Horse killed?

Larger than Life

16   Most people choose their life's work. But sometimes a task seems to choose a person. That's what happened to Korczak Ziolkowski [Core'chock Jew·el·cuff'skee]. Both of his parents, who were Polish immigrants, had died by the time he was a year old. He grew up in a foster home. He never

had an art lesson in his life. But, in 1939, he won a major prize for his sculpture. He also came to Mount Rushmore to work with Borglum briefly. Later that year, Sioux Chief Henry Standing Bear wrote to the young sculptor. "The red man has great heroes, too," he said. He invited Ziolkowski to carve a statue of Crazy Horse in the Black Hills. Ziolkowski felt honored.

17   After World War II, Ziolkowski returned to South Dakota to begin this incredible task. Thunderhead Mountain would have an enormous figure of Crazy Horse, no matter how long it took. "Every man has his mountain," Ziolkowski said. "I'm carving mine." Crazy Horse had once told his people that he would return to them in stone. Now, with Ziolkowski's help, he would.

18   The statue was to tell this story: A white hunter taunted[4] Crazy Horse, "Where are your lands now?" Crazy Horse pointed east and replied, "My lands are where my dead lie buried." Ziolkowski's design recreates this moment.

19   From 1949 to 1982, this storyteller in stone blasted more than seven million tons of rock from Thunderhead. But Crazy Horse did not emerge. On his deathbed, Ziolkowski told his wife and 10 children, "Crazy Horse must be finished . . . but go slowly, so you do it right." He gave about 35 years of his life to the monument. He hoped that Crazy Horse would be a source of Indian pride. The memorial's goals include an Indian cultural center and a university and medical training center for Indians.

Checking Comprehension

Whose idea was it to have a mountain carving of Crazy Horse?

Why is Ziolkowski called a storyteller in stone?

---

[4]teased in a cruel way

20   Following Ziolkowski's three books of instructions and using his scale models, family members have continued his dream. In 1991, Crazy Horse's head appeared. With luck, the face will be completed by the year 2000. Ziolkowski's family can't say when the entire sculpture will be finished. Sometimes bad weather limits work to only five months a year. And financing is always a question mark. It could take another 50 to 100 years, but Ziolkowski's family is determined to finish the job.

21   Someday the great chief and his horse will stand in the round,[5] 563 feet high and 641 feet long. Crazy Horse's head will be 90 feet high. The outstretched arm will be almost as long as a football field, long enough for 4,000 people to stand on. The horse's head will be 22 stories high. A five-room house could fit in each nostril! It will, of course, be the largest sculpture in the world.

Workers bringing Crazy Horse's nine-story-high face to life

---

[5]in full sculptured form and not attached to a background

22   As the work goes on, more than a million tourists a year stop by to watch. They also visit the Indian Museum of North America (run by Ziolkowski's daughter) and the sculptor's studio. Admission fees plus private donations are paying for the nonprofit educational and cultural memorial. Ziolkowski twice refused offers of $10 million in government funding.

23   What keeps a person working so hard for so long on a very difficult, almost endless task? Here's how Ziolkowski explained it: "The world asks you one question, 'Did you do your job?' The answer is not, 'I would have done it if the people had been nicer . . . if I'd had the money . . . if I hadn't died.' Ifs don't count. The answer must be, 'Yes!' " This is the spirit that carves mountains.

Checking Comprehension

Why is the Crazy Horse statue taking longer to carve than the Mount Rushmore heads?

What did Ziolkowski mean by "Ifs don't count"?

SIDELIGHTS

About Mount Rushmore

- A Rushmore head is the perfect size—for a person 465 feet tall!
- The opening in Lincoln's eye is large enough for a child to lie down in.
- On a clear day, the Mount Rushmore heads can be seen for 62 miles.

About Crazy Horse

Does the Crazy Horse sculpture look like the great Indian leader? No one knows. Ziolkowski sculpted the spirit and not the features of the man because no photograph existed. Once, when a white man asked to take his picture, Crazy Horse replied, "What? Would you imprison my shadow, too?"

Crazy Horse's original name was Curly. His father's name was Crazy Horse. But his father was so proud of his son that he gave him the greatest gift he had—his good name.

About South Dakota

South Dakota is called the land of infinite variety because of its beautiful and varied landscape. This includes the famous Badlands, an area of sandy hills and gullies with strange shapes. The state has lakes and rolling hills formed by glaciers. This beautiful area was home to Wild Bill Hickock, Calamity Jane, and other figures of the Wild West. The geographic center of the United States (including Alaska and Hawaii) lies in South Dakota, near Castle Rock.

Making Inferences

*Reread the paragraph(s) indicated after each statement.
Then decide if each statement is probably true or false.*

_____ 1. The Crazy Horse Memorial is more closely
related to South Dakota's history than the Mount
Rushmore National Memorial is. (paragraphs 2,
13, 14)
_____ 2. Borglum and Ziolkowski were both born in the
United States. They were native Americans but
not Native Americans. (paragraphs 2, 16)
_____ 3. Neither Borglum nor Ziolkowski saw the
completed mountain carving he designed.
(paragraphs 9, 19)
_____ 4. The families of these sculptors considered their
work important. (paragraphs 9, 19)
_____ 5. Ziolkowski approved of the way the American
government had treated Native Americans.
(paragraph 19)

Practicing Vocabulary

*What does each phrase in italics mean in this reading?
Reread the paragraphs. Then circle the correct answer.*

1. In paragraph 3, *representative government* means that
   (a) the people who control the government are elected
   by the citizens (b) all the citizens have equal rights.
2. In paragraph 3, a *permanent union*
   (a) will last forever (b) will be temporary.
3. In paragraph 5, *regional heroes* are
   (a) well known all over the nation (b) famous in a
   particular area of the country.

4. In paragraph 9, *private donations* means
   (a) money that didn't come from the government (b) secret donations.
5. In paragraph 10, *breathtaking* means
   (a) it can kill you (b) it's beautiful and thrilling.

Talking It Over

1. Should a lot of money be spent on carving sculpture into mountains? Would it be better to spend that money helping the poor?
2. Compare the Mount Rushmore and the Crazy Horse sculptures. In what ways are they similar? What are some differences?
3. For what reasons do you think Ziolkowski refused to let the American government finance the Crazy Horse Memorial?
4. If someone decided to add another head to Mount Rushmore, what famous person would you suggest?
5. Korczak Ziolkowski has been quoted as saying, "Every man has his mountain—I'm carving mine." What "mountain" are you trying to carve?
6. Have you ever tried to do something that everyone said was impossible? Did you succeed? Are you still trying to do it?
7. Crazy Horse was killed on September 6. Ziolkowski was born on that same day of the year. How do you think Ziolkowski might have felt about this coincidence? Have you had any unusual coincidences in your life?

A view of the Grand Canyon

HISTORY IN STONE

The Grand Canyon's North and South Rims are only 10 miles apart. But to get from one side to the other by car, it would take about four hours. Sound incredible? Read on. . . .

A Master Stonecutter

1   Arizona's Grand Canyon is one of the world's largest barriers.[1] It measures 279 miles long, 13 miles at its widest, and over 1 mile deep. Who carved this great natural wonder? You could say that nature did. Or, you could say that the mighty Colorado River cut this beautiful stone canyon. This happened after the Rocky Mountains rose out of the earth. The process by which the Colorado River cut rock and made the Grand Canyon is called *erosion*, a slow process that removes or reshapes rocky material. Nowhere are its results better seen than at the Grand Canyon.

2   In the walls of the Grand Canyon, there is a billion-year-old picture of life on earth. Some of the world's oldest fossils[2] can be found here. Ancient plants and animals

---

[1]boundaries or limits, things that prevent passage
[2]impressions in stone of a skeleton, leaf print, or footprint

without backbones that no longer live on earth are preserved in these walls. Like a museum, the Grand Canyon's walls tell us about life in the past. Looking at the fossils, we can see how life on earth has changed. This helps scientists to understand life today.

3   Every year, more than four million tourists visit the Grand Canyon. Most of them visit the South Rim. They hike, camp, ride horses, go rafting, or drive on the many scenic roads. Nearly every year, a few unlucky visitors lose their footing and take what locals call the 12-second tour. But danger is not the problem at the Grand Canyon. Rather, the problem is how to take in so much beauty on one visit. Most visitors would agree with John Wesley Powell, the early explorer of the Colorado River and the Grand Canyon. He said of the Grand Canyon, "Its colors, though many and complex at any instant, change with the ascending and declining sun. . . . You cannot see the Grand Canyon in one view."

Tourists viewing the Grand Canyon from its South Rim

4   Powell was not the first person to visit the Grand Canyon. For thousands of years, many Indian tribes, including the Havasupai [Have·u·sue'pie] ("people of the blue-green water"), have lived in the Grand Canyon. They lived there long before white men arrived. They were farmers, who used the water of the Colorado River to cultivate[3] their crops. They lived beside waterfalls. They gathered wild foods and firewood from the beautiful canyon.

5   Another tribe that lived at a distant edge or rim of the Grand Canyon was the Anasazi [On·u·sah'zee] Indians. They were hunters. They hunted the wildlife there, which included deer, bighorn sheep, and rabbits. They also made pottery and wove beautiful baskets. These bowls and baskets can be seen in many museums in the West today.

Checking Comprehension

In what way is the Grand Canyon a barrier?

What was the master stonecutter of the Grand Canyon?

What can the walls of the Grand Canyon tell us about life
    on earth?

---

[3]to nurture and grow

6   The first explorers of the Grand Canyon were not interested in baskets, bowls, farming, or fossils. In 1540, Spanish explorers, led by Francisco Coronado [Core·oh·nah'dough], came in search of gold and riches. They found no gold. But the Hopi Indians, who lived near the canyon, led one of Coronado's men, Garcia Lopez de Cardenas [day Car'duh·nus], to a greater wonder. They led him to the Grand Canyon itself. Many years later, silver was discovered in this region. Then another Spanish explorer, Juan de Oñate [Own·yaht'tay], said that the Southwest, including the Grand Canyon, belonged to Spain.

7   Fur trappers probably visited the Grand Canyon in the 1820s. But the first American to really explore the Grand Canyon was a one-armed army major. His name was John Wesley Powell. In 1869, he set out from Wyoming. He took four rowboats and nine men to navigate[4] the Colorado River. Powell plunged over waterfalls and ran the rapids[5] of the big river. The river has 70 major rapids! He also made many maps and drawings of the rocks, the plants, the animals, and the abandoned[6] Indian sites. He liked the Grand Canyon so much that he returned two years later. His reports made people want to see the Colorado River and the Grand Canyon for themselves. In 1883, the tourist trade really began when a four-room hotel opened at Diamond Creek.

8   Explorers, miners, and Indians all lived together in and around the Grand Canyon during the late 1800s. But it is a difficult place to live. Often it is too hot or too cold. There is little rainfall and not much good farmland. So, there

---

[4]to explore a river
[5]steered a boat through a fast-moving part of a river
[6]left behind, not inhabited by people

have never been more than 3,200 people living in the immediate area. A group of Mormons settled in this remote place in the 1860s. They were ranchers who tended sheep together. They shared the same religious beliefs. Their beliefs included a form of polygamy in which the men could have more than one wife. This practice made them unpopular with the other residents, so they built Windsor Castle. It was a ranch with high walls that protected them from the outside world. They named it after the famous castle in England, where the queen stays outside London. Its strange design and odd name made it popular with tourists as well. This "castle" no longer exists.

Checking Comprehension

Why did the first Spanish explorers visit the Grand Canyon?

Who was John Wesley Powell?

Why were the Mormons unpopular with the other Grand Canyon residents?

A National Monument

9   In 1908, President Theodore Roosevelt made the Grand Canyon a national monument. Today, it is a protected area taken care of by the U.S. government. In 1975, the borders of the Grand Canyon Wilderness Park were extended. The area now includes more land to the west and northeast. The extensions doubled the size of the Grand Canyon Wilderness Park. Also, several wilderness reserves[7] were created to protect wildlife and the many forests within the park.

---

[7]places where plants and animals are protected

10   Visitors to the Grand Canyon today enter at the south or east entrance. An admission fee of $10 per vehicle is charged for a week's stay. Tourist attractions at the park include a 26-mile scenic drive, a geology museum, Indian ruins, and Desert View.

11   Desert View is a scenic overlook.[8] From it, the Painted Desert is visible with its pink, orange, yellow, and gray stripes. The Painted Desert is a rocky area covered with pine trees and cactus, not the sandy place most people picture when thinking of a desert. This flat desert is 7,500 feet above sea level.

12   The Desert View Watchtower is also located in this area. Built in 1932 by covering a steel frame with stone, this building looks both prehistoric[9] and modern at the same time. In addition to wall paintings and a Hopi Indian altar,[10] this 70-foot building has a snack bar, a general store, and even a gas station.

13   Only 1 out of every 10 visitors sees the North Rim of the Canyon. It is difficult to reach and is open only from mid-May to October. Here, tourists can photograph beautiful wildflowers. Hikers can also wander through large forests. In winter, some people with special permission ski in this isolated area. About 10 miles straight across from the North Rim is the South Rim. By foot, the distance is 22 miles. By car, a driver would have to drive 215 miles around to get from one rim to the other! No wonder the Grand Canyon is called a natural barrier.

14   To visit the park as the prospectors did, some people hire a mule. But a mule trip to the bottom of the canyon is not for everyone. The ride follows Bright Angel Trail over a steep path. Mule riders must stay in the saddle all day and cross a bridge over a river. A rider must be in good health,

---

[8]a place with a good view of nature
[9]before history began, very old
[10]place where people pray

weigh less than 200 pounds, and be over 4 feet 7 inches tall. A hat that ties under the chin, long pants, long sleeves, and closed shoes are required. Riders cannot carry bags, backpacks, or purses, but they can carry cameras. If they would like to bring luggage, they can hire another mule to carry it in and out for $60. At the bottom of the canyon, mule riders can stay overnight at Phantom Ranch.

15   For a bird's-eye view of the Grand Canyon, some tourists rent an airplane or helicopter. About 40 different companies operate such flights. These flights can be as short as 30 minutes or as long as a 100-minute grand tour for $115 (that's $1.15 a minute). A person can also take a sunrise or sunset helicopter flight over the Grand Canyon.

A Grand Canyon Railway steam train carrying visitors to the Canyon from its South Rim

Checking Comprehension

How is the Painted Desert unlike most deserts?

How can you see the Grand Canyon without a car?

What's unusual about the location of the Canyon's North Rim and South Rim?

Arizona's Other Sights

16   Besides the Grand Canyon, Arizona is the home of other spectacular sights. The Petrified Forest National Park contains the world's biggest collection of petrified wood (wood that has turned to rock) in the world. Trees that are over 225 million years old and are buried under sand and clay have turned into brightly colored stone. One such famous stone is Newspaper Rock. Here Indians drew pictures thousands of years ago. In 1906, President Theodore Roosevelt made the Petrified Forest a national monument.

17   Ancient animal fossils have been saved at the Petrified Forest too. These include animals that swam underwater millions of years ago. They tell the changing story of the region. Today, this area of Arizona is no longer under water. In fact, it's very dry, averaging only nine inches of rainfall a year.

18   Among the fossils in the Petrified Forest is Gertie. That's the name scientists have given to one of the oldest dinosaur skeletons discovered in North America. Gertie roamed the forest 225 million years ago. She was a type of giant alligator called a phytosaur [fight'oh·sore].

19   In the late 1800s, the Petrified Forest was damaged by tourists. They took away much of the beautiful petrified wood. They removed the shiny crystals stuck inside it. Perhaps to protect the wood, a superstition arose. Anyone who carried wood away from the Petrified Forest was supposed to have bad luck. Maybe the superstition worked. Within the Petrified Forest today, visitors can see the Conscience Wood Exhibit. Here, hundreds of pieces of returned wood are displayed along with letters of apology.

20   Another wonder of this state might best be seen on a map. This is Four Corners Monument. It is the only place in the United States where a tourist can stand in four states at once! A beautiful new monument marks the spot where

New Mexico, Utah, Colorado, and Arizona meet. More than 2,000 tourists a day visit this site in summer. They buy items such as jewelry, baskets, pottery, and rugs from Indian souvenir booths.

Checking Comprehension

What is petrified in the Petrified Forest?

Who is Gertie?

What four states come together at the Four Corners Monument?

Star 48

21   Most Americans know that the states of Alaska and Hawaii were the 49th and 50th to be added to the American flag. But what was the 48th? It was Arizona, which entered the Union in 1912, after a stormy history of ownership. First, there was an Indian civilization dating as far back as 15,000 years ago. The early Indians who lived there were hunters. We know that from the spears they left behind.

22   After thousands of years of rich Indian history, Spanish missionaries[11] and explorers arrived. There were reports of cities of gold, but no gold was discovered by the early Spaniards. The Spanish missionaries did set up several large missions among the Hopi Indians, who lived in pueblos, flat-roofed stone or mud-covered houses. In 1680, relations turned from friendly to hostile. Indians living in an area that is now New Mexico led a revolt, killed the missionaries, and destroyed some of the missions in the Pueblo Uprising.

---

[11]ministers and priests sent to teach religion

23   In 1821, Mexico became free from Spain. Arizona became part of the new country of Mexico. If there hadn't been a war between Mexico and the United States (1846–1848), Arizona might never have joined the Union. But Mexico lost the war in 1848, and Arizona was given to the United States in an agreement called the Treaty of Guadalupe [Gwa·duh·loo'pay] Hidalgo.

24   During the Civil War, there was more trouble in Arizona. Some settlers who lived in southern Arizona were friendly to the slave-holding Southern states. There were fights between citizens who backed the North and those who supported the South. In 1862, Confederate President Jefferson Davis claimed that Arizona was a Confederate territory. President Abraham Lincoln quickly signed a bill to make Arizona an American territory on February 24, 1863. Many years later, Arizona became a state. Its first governor was George W. P. Hunt. A successful businessman, he had come to the state as an unemployed miner in 1881. In 1912, he led the celebration as the United States added star 48.

Checking Comprehension

How did the Civil War affect Arizona?

When did Arizona's status change from U.S. territory to state?

SIDELIGHTS

About the Grand Canyon

- It's one of the most visited parks in the United States.
- Half a million tourists a year come from outside this country.
- Layers of the Canyon's exposed rock are purple, red, green, brown, and orange.
- 50,000 sight-seeing flights a year explore the Grand Canyon.

About Arizona (the Grand Canyon State)

Arizona is one of our fastest-growing states. Its warm, dry climate and plentiful sunshine are good for your health. For these reasons, many retired people among others have flocked to Arizona. In the last 20 years, the population has increased by 2 million. It's now about 3.6 million.

The Colorado River is Arizona's greatest water source. It flows through 688 miles of the state, 277 of which are in the Grand Canyon.

Though called the Grand Canyon State, Arizona might be called the recreation state. It has 20 national parklands, 7 national forests, 21 state parks, and more than 100 museums.

Making Inferences

Reread the paragraph(s) indicated after each statement. Then decide if each statement is probably true or false.

_____ 1. Erosion continues to change the Grand Canyon. (paragraph 1)

_____ 2. The Havasupai Indians were friends and neighbors of the Anasazi Indians. (paragraphs 4–5)

_____ 3. John Wesley Powell was not a brave man. (paragraph 7)

_____ 4. You could get a flat tire fixed at Desert View Watchtower. (paragraph 12)

_____ 5. Millions of years ago, parts of Arizona were under water. (paragraph 17)

Practicing Vocabulary

Choose five of the following eight words to complete the sentences.

barrier	**firewood**	**rapids**	**superstition**
erosion	**fossils**	**steep**	**waterfalls**

1. The process of _____ made the Grand Canyon.

2. The Grand Canyon is a great natural _____.

3. Many _____ are preserved in the walls of the Grand Canyon.

4. Major Powell ran the _____ when he explored the Grand Canyon's Colorado River.

5. He saw many beautiful sights, including _____.

Talking It Over

1. Suppose you are taking a trip to the Grand Canyon. Plan two lists: (1) things to take along on the trip and (2) things to see.
2. Should people have one spouse at a time or practice polygamy, like the Mormons who settled near the Grand Canyon?
3. Of all the methods of transportation available, what method would you choose to tour the Grand Canyon? Why?
4. Did President Theodore Roosevelt care about nature? How do you know?
5. What superstitions do you believe in? Why do you think people invent superstitions like the one about the petrified wood?

*Mickey and Minnie Mouse shrubbery framing entrance of
Magic Kingdom*

DISNEY'S WORLD

Walt Disney World is the world's largest amusement resort. How big is it? To find the answer, read on. . . .

Happiness for Sale

1 For many years, Orlando, Florida, was a quiet place. It was known mostly for its sunshine and oranges. In 1950, its population was about 52,000. Today, about 1 million people make the Orlando area their home. In addition, Orlando attracts 13 million visitors a year! What happened? The answer is simple: Walt Disney World arrived.

2 The story of Walt Disney World began in the early 1940s. At that time, Walt Disney was a famous movie producer. He was also a loving father of two little girls. He often took his daughters to amusement parks. The parks were dirty, smelly, run-down places with bad food. Disney thought that kids and their parents deserved better. He decided to build a park that the whole family could enjoy. The result was the 1955 opening of Disneyland in Anaheim, California. It was the first large amusement park to combine rides, exhibits, and shows around major themes.

3 Disneyland's great success encouraged Walt Disney. He wanted more space to develop more ideas. On the other side of the country, central Florida had year-round nice weather and cheap land. In 1964, Walt Disney began buying land just southwest of Orlando. By 1965, the company

had spent $5.5 million and purchased 43 square miles—an area twice the size of Manhattan and almost 150 times larger than Disneyland. Today, Walt Disney World is the world's largest vacation resort.

4   Walt Disney wanted to share his belief that life was a wonderful adventure. He wanted his parks to give visitors imaginative fun in a beautiful, clean, friendly place. One day in Disneyland, Walt heard an employee speaking rudely to some guests. He called over the man's boss and told him, "See if you can't cheer him up. If he feels sour, he shouldn't work here. We are selling happiness."

5   At Disney parks, everything is created in great detail. The rides are not just rides. Passengers go to the Caribbean, a haunted house, a jungle, or outer space. The outdoor shows often include fireworks, thousands of electric lights, and sometimes lasers to brighten the night sky.

6   Today, Walt Disney World has three main theme parks: the Magic Kingdom, EPCOT Center, and the Disney-MGM Studios Theme Park. It also has the world's largest water park. Typhoon Lagoon has water slides almost 100 feet high and a pond with waves big enough to surf on. Then there are nature preserves and exhibits, lakes, golf courses, hotels, restaurants, and nightclubs. In 1989, Pleasure Island opened. This man-made island has theme nightclubs, movie theaters, restaurants, and shops.

7   Visitors get around the area on its highways, elevated monorail trains, and waterways. Since it opened in 1971, over 400 million people have come to Walt Disney World.

Checking Comprehension

Why did Walt Disney create Disneyland?
Why did he choose to locate Disney World in Florida?

---

8   The Magic Kingdom has more than 40 attractions in seven different sections. Just walking around the Magic Kingdom is fun. The old-fashioned Main Street is crowded with performers, some dressed like famous Disney cartoon characters. Bushes are even shaped to look like Mickey and Minnie Mouse. Most of the attractions are based on Disney cartoon characters and Disney movies.

9   Cinderella Castle is the most familiar symbol of the Magic Kingdom. It's also one of the most beautiful Disney buildings. The outside looks like a real French castle from the Middle Ages. Inside are huge mosaics.[1] They tell the story of Cinderella's rise from rags to riches.

*Floral arrangement marking Walt Disney World's
20th anniversary*

Used by Permission of © The Walt Disney Company

---

[1]pictures made of small pieces of colored stone or glass

10   In the Hall of Presidents, all the U.S. presidents appear on stage. These life-sized figures can move. Some even talk. Abraham Lincoln, for example, can give speeches. He can also make 49 different motions and 15 different facial expressions. These amazing figures (which Disney calls *Audio-Animatronics*) are part of many attractions.

11   In "It's a Small World," visitors ride by boat past more than 500 moving dolls dressed in the traditional clothing of many different nations. Passengers leave the ride humming the tune. They also carry away the song's message. The clothes may be different, but people are people.

EPCOT Center

12   EPCOT Center opened in 1982. The letters stand for Experimental Prototype[2] Community of Tomorrow. This park didn't turn out as Disney first imagined it. His dream was of a real town where new ways of living could be tested. But EPCOT is an exciting and educational place to visit. And it does deal with what is new and experimental.

13   EPCOT is divided into two main sections—Future World and World Showcase. Future World contains the famous symbol of EPCOT, the 17-story Spaceship Earth. While traveling to the top of this huge ball, visitors see and hear about the history of communication from cave paintings to computers. Future World has nine pavilions,[3] showing the past, present, and future of technology. Movies, TV, rides, exhibits, and Audio-Animatronics teach about the sea and land, the human body and nutrition, and the importance of imagination.

14   In 1986, the Living Seas aquarium opened at EPCOT Center. Holding 5.7 million gallons of water, it's the largest aquarium in the world. It's so large that Spaceship Earth

---

[2]an experimental model
[3]buildings used for exhibits

could fit inside it. In the Living Seas pavilion, visitors begin by viewing a short film. It stresses the importance of the ocean as a source of energy. After the film, they board gondolas[4] and ride through an underwater viewing tunnel. On their journey through this tunnel, they see about 200 kinds of marine life. These include stingrays, dolphins, barracuda, sharks, and—what's this?—Mickey Mouse in scuba-diving gear! But that shouldn't be surprising. In Walt Disney World, Mickey Mouse is everywhere.

Seventeen-story Spaceship Earth at EPCOT Center

15　　　Visitors can walk or take a ferryboat ride to get from Future World to World Showcase. Here, pavilions feature 11 countries and their typical native foods, products, and entertainment. These countries are Canada, China, France, Germany, Italy, Japan, Mexico, Morocco, Norway, the United Kingdom, and the United States. In the "American Adventure" show, 35 Audio-Animatronics figures tell the story of the nation's history.

Checking Comprehension

What are Audio-Animatronics?
Are Walt Disney World attractions educational?
What is in the Living Seas aquarium?

---

[4]long, narrow flat-bottomed boats

The Disney-MGM Studios Theme Park

16   In 1989, the Disney-MGM Studios Theme Park opened just south of EPCOT Center. This park is about the same size as the Magic Kingdom, about half the size of EPCOT. The letters *MGM* stand for Metro-Goldwyn-Mayer. Disney obtained the rights to use not only the MGM name but also its film library, titles, costumes, music, and sets. So, two major filmmakers—MGM and Disney—are showcased.

17   This theme park is a real working movie and TV production facility. The rides, shows, and exhibits are all about movie and TV production. Various attractions teach visitors how sound effects and animated films are made. But visitors who come for recreation, not education, also enjoy this park—especially its stunt show and rides. On the simulated[5] rides, chairs shake as passengers watch a 3-D movie. Soon they're off on a great adventure, traveling "through" the places on the screen.

Who Tours Walt Disney World?

18   Walt Disney World is open to almost everyone. Visitors can rent strollers and wheelchairs. People who don't speak English well can still enjoy the beautiful and unusual sights. Also, foreign language tapes and guides help tourists whose main language is not English.

19   In a single day, 15,000 to 150,000 tourists may visit Walt Disney World. People keep coming—and coming back—because there are always new things to see. To avoid long lines, it's best to avoid the most popular vacation times: late December, Easter, and summer. Even during less

---

[5]made to feel or look like the real thing

crowded times, it takes at least a day to see the highlights of each park. Visitors looking for bargains buy the four-day Walt Disney World ticket. That pays for all the sights in the three main parks, and visitors can come and go as many times as they want. For further savings, tourists stay in the reasonably priced motels and campgrounds outside Walt Disney World. With careful planning, it's possible to spend a week at Walt Disney World without also spending a fortune.

20   There's a saying at Walt Disney World—"If you can dream it, you can do it." Walt Disney was never afraid to risk his money and his reputation on a new idea. "It's kind of fun to do the impossible," he said. Walt Disney died in 1966. But his ideas are still entertaining the world. Mickey Mouse visited China in 1986 as Mi Lao Shu. He went to Russia in 1988. In Japan, Tokyo Disneyland opened in 1983. Euro Disney, 20 miles from Paris, opened in 1992. For that occasion, Mickey learned to say *bienvenue* [bi·yen·ven·oo']⁶ to give everyone a warm French welcome to the world of Disney.

Checking Comprehension

At what time of the year is Walt Disney World most
    crowded?

What foreign countries have Disney theme parks?

---

⁶welcome (French)

Beyond Walt Disney World

21   Outside the Disney complex, central Florida has dozens of other tourist sites. At Sea World, whales, dolphins, and other animals put on daily shows. Visitors also see the world's largest collection of dangerous marine animals such as sharks and poisonous fish. Universal Studios (like Disney-MGM Studios) is a real movie studio and a theme park with rides and shows. Gatorland Zoo houses thousands of alligators. Some entertain tourists by jumping five feet into the air to grab a whole chicken from a trainer's hands. Other alligators are raised for their meat. The gift shop sells cans of Gator Chowder.

Blast Off!

22   Cape Canaveral, about 90 minutes east of Walt Disney World, is another place where dreams become reality. It's the Kennedy Space Center, the main launch site for American spacecraft. Its location on the eastern edge of the country is ideal. Rockets are fired toward the ocean. If something goes wrong, local residents, visitors, and property are not hurt. Also, because the earth travels from west to east, vehicles launched eastward over the ocean get a running start of about 1,000 miles per hour.

23   After the Soviet Union sent a person into space in 1961, President John F. Kennedy announced that the United States should send someone to the moon by 1970. The National Aeronautics and Space Administration (NASA) beat Kennedy's deadline. On July 16, 1969, three American astronauts left Kennedy Space Center headed for the moon. Four days later, they arrived. While their spaceship circled the moon, two astronauts took a lunar landing vehicle to the moon's surface. Neil Armstrong was the first

person to walk on the moon. His message to earth was, "That's one small step for a man, one giant leap for mankind."

24   Tourists are welcome to visit Cape Canaveral. At the space center, bus tours show visitors the launching areas, the equipment that transports and holds space vehicles, and the huge building where spaceships are put together. Space suits, moon rocks, rockets, and lunar modules are displayed. While at Cape Canaveral, many tourists also visit its wildlife refuge,[7] which has the largest number of endangered animals in the country.

Spaceship loaded on a transport at Cape Canaveral

---

[7]a place where protection from danger is provided

25   The U.S. space program has many practical benefits. For example, some satellites[8] gather weather information and warn of dangerous conditions. Others send TV, radio, telephone, and other communications all over the world with great speed. American scientists and scientists from 13 other countries are building a permanent space station. It will circle the earth 250 miles from its surface. By the year 2000, eight people will live and work there for months at a time, doing important research. In the 21st century, adventurous travelers may also be able to vacation on the moon or even Mars. But for now, central Florida and Walt Disney World remain the world's most popular destinations for vacationing.

Checking Comprehension

What are some of central Florida's other tourist sites?
Why do tourists come to Cape Canaveral?
What are endangered animals?

---

[8]man-made objects circling the earth

SIDELIGHTS

About the Disney Company

- Number of employees: 54,800
- Revenue for 1992: $6.1 billion

About Walt Disney World

- Number of employees: 32,000
- Best time of year to go: September through mid-December. Average crowds then are a mere 25,000 visitors per day! Summer crowds average 60,000 daily.
- Most unusual fan: Jim Jones has 57 Disney characters tattooed on his 326-pound body.

About Kennedy Space Center

- heaviest object ever sent into orbit: 309,690 pounds
- longest object ever sent into orbit: 1,500 feet
- fastest speed an astronaut ever traveled: 24,791 miles per hour

About Florida (the Sunshine State)

Florida has more than 1,350 miles of coastline—more than any other state except Alaska. It also has the most subtropical wilderness areas. Of the 50 states, Florida is 22nd in size and 4th in population. About 13 million people live there, and another 40 million come to vacation. Many visitors go home with a bag of citrus fruit. Florida is the leading producer of oranges, grapefruits, and tangerines.

Making Inferences

Reread the paragraph(s) indicated after each statement. Then decide if each statement is probably true or false.

_____ 1. Walt Disney World always closes before dark. (paragraph 5)

_____ 2. Most tourists visit all three of the Disney main parks in one day. (paragraph 19)

_____ 3. The Kennedy Space Center is a large airport in Orlando. (paragraph 22)

_____ 4. A wildlife refuge is a place where animals can live safely. (paragraph 24)

_____ 5. The space program is exciting, but it doesn't really improve life for the ordinary person. (paragraph 25)

Practicing Vocabulary

Complete the following paragraph with any appropriate words. Then rewrite it using some of the words listed after the paragraph.

1. Life can be exciting if you let your imagination be your _____. 2. When you use your _____, any kind of adventure is possible. 3. In your fantasy, you can become an _____ and _____ off into outer space. 4. There is no risk in taking an imaginary journey to the moon or orbiting the earth in a _____. 5. You don't need to worry about good _____ because you can squeeze a lot of healthy foods out of tubes. 6. Best of all, you can come back to good old planet _____ any time you want.

7. When you take an imaginary trip, you are the
_____, director, and star of the _____
you have imagined.

adventure	**earth**	**nutrition**	**satellite**
astronaut	**guide**	**orbit**	**theme**
blast	**imagination**	**producer**	

Talking It Over

1. What are some of the themes of Walt Disney World?
2. If you have ever visited a theme park, describe it and point out its location on a map. How much did it cost to get in? Do you recommend that others visit it? Was it worth the price?
3. What advice do you have for people going to theme parks? What warnings?
4. Walt Disney World's word for moving figures, *Audio-Animatronics*, is a trademark. What is a trademark? Can you name some words for American products that are trademarks?
5. In your opinion, is the manned space program a worthwhile investment for the United States?

ANSWER KEY

Making Inferences, page 14
1. False. The inside has an iron skeleton, but it is not solid. There are stairways inside.
2. True.
3. True. Americans gave millions for her restoration. Also, they come by the millions each year to visit her. But in the 1880s, they were slow to contribute money for the building of the pedestal.
4. False. They did not have the right to vote at the time.
5. False. Most immigrants were worried about the Ellis Island inspection and they were frightened even after they passed the inspection. Starting a new life was scary.
6. False. Many Ellis Island immigrants are no longer alive. But many visitors are their children and grandchildren.

Practicing Vocabulary, page 14
Part A.
All the words except *embarrassing* and *exhausting* mean very big.
Part B.
1. pedestal
2. exhausting
3. torch
4. restore
5. popular

Talking It Over, page 15
1. The cartoon was a plea for money to build the pedestal.
2. Contributors to the pedestal were listed in a newspaper. Contributors to a special fund for Ellis Island could have their ancestors' names listed on a wall for Ellis Island immigrants.
3. Answers will vary. Some historians think he maintained the secret in order to keep people interested and guessing about it.
4. Answers will vary. Some think that, even in the United States, women do not always have equal opportunities in the business world. In many other nations, women are controlled first by their fathers and then by their husbands.

5. Answers will vary. Some people think that a multi-ethnic statue would be more appropriate now. Some may think that a more abstract design would be more fitting.
6. In the 1920s and 1930s, entertainers and athletes referred to the city as the Big Apple. The idea was that there are a lot of apples in a tree, and New York City was like the biggest and best one at the top. To those in the public eye, success in New York City was considered the highest achievement. In 1971, the New York Convention and Visitors Bureau made the saying a part of its marketing theme, so, today, it's very well known.

SKY HIGH

Making Inferences, page 26
1. False. He wanted to get started before he was seen. He knew he couldn't reach the top before daybreak. He wanted to be seen, but not until after he was too high to be stopped.
2. False. Their biggest worry was that Goodwin would fall off and kill himself.
3. True.
4. True.
5. True. The John Hancock Center is the tallest multi-purpose skyscraper in the city.

Practicing Vocabulary, pages 26–27
1. boast
2. skyscrapers
3. sight-seers or spectators
4. elevator
5. skyline, high-rise

Talking It Over, page 27
1. Every skyscraper is a high rise, but not every high rise is a skyscraper. A high rise is a building tall enough to require an elevator. Nowadays, in the United States, the term *skyscraper* is used for buildings that are at least 40 stories. In some other countries, a building shorter than that is considered a skyscraper.
2. Answers will vary.
3. Answers will vary.
4. Dan Goodwin is a person who likes to take risks, who finds danger exciting, and who enjoys attention. Some

appropriate adjectives are *brave, courageous, daring, athletic, energetic*, and *self-confident*. Some people might also describe him as foolish or foolhardy or as a showoff.

5. Answers will vary.
6. Answers will vary.

GATEWAY TO THE WEST

Making Inferences, page 40

1. True. His design was beautiful, but he needed help from engineers to make the arch stable.
2. False. The Constitution didn't say that the government could buy land, but it didn't say that it couldn't, either.
3. False. They went because President Jefferson asked them to.
4. False. Most of the people who went West were poor people looking for ways to make more money.
5. True. The Gold Rush attracted people to California.

Practicing Vocabulary, pages 40–41
Part A.

1. architect   5. guides
2. pioneer   6. miners
3. explorers   7. cowboys
4. pioneers
Part B.
4, 2, 5, 3, 1

Talking It Over, page 41

1. To Americans today, the golden arches of McDonald's (the fast-food restaurant) may be the most famous arches of all. But the most well-known standing arch in the Western world is the Arc de Triomphe in Paris, France. It stands in the Place Charles de Gaulle where 12 avenues meet. It is about 164 feet high. Napoleon began building this arch in 1806 to honor his troops. Although the arch as an architectural form was known in ancient Egypt and Greece, the Romans were the first to use it in monumental architecture.
2. Answers will vary. Examples of Americans' pioneering spirit might be outer space exploration and computer technology development.
3. Answers will vary.
4. Native Americans can now live on or off reservations, whichever they choose. There are now about 2 million Native Americans living within the United States. Their

standard of living and life expectancy are quite low compared to other Americans, but conditions and opportunities are gradually improving for them.

5. Answers will vary. Some people think that most American movies have romanticized the West, but that others have been realistic. For example, movie cowboys usually look handsome, clean, and neat. Photographs of cowboys show much less glamorous figures.

HEADS OF STATE

Making Inferences, page 54

1. True. The Crazy Horse Memorial, a tribute to the Sioux, is on land that used to be theirs.

2. True. A Native American is an American Indian. A native American is a person born in the United States.

3. True. Both men died leaving their sculptures unfinished. Their children continued their work.

4. True. Borglum's son Lincoln worked on Rushmore until the money ran out. Several of Ziolkowski's children are involved in the mountain carving and other jobs related to the Crazy Horse Memorial.

5. False. Ziolkowski felt very bad about the treatment and conditions that American Indians have endured. He wanted his sculpture to help them regain their lost pride. He also wanted money earned by the site to be spent on humanitarian efforts to help Indians improve their lives.

Practicing Vocabulary, page 54

1. a   2. a   3. b   4. a   5. b

Talking It Over, page 55

1. Answers will vary. Some people think that a mountain carving can be an amazing artistic and engineering achievement that is thrilling for people to see and that it can help people take pride in their heritage and/or remember an important person, event, or accomplishment. In addition, a mountain carving attracts tourists, so it brings in revenue that can be used for humanitarian purposes. Others believe that carving into mountains alters the natural beauty of the landscape and costs a lot of money that could be used to help people in need. Because it is outdoors, it deteriorates when attacked by the elements. In addition, it takes a long time to complete. Instead of

carving one mountain sculpture for many years, a sculptor could produce many artistic works on a smaller scale.

2. Some similarities are that both were carved in granite by the use of dynamite and drills, and both were created by first making a model and then enlarging the model many times. Some differences are that Crazy Horse will be carved in the round. The Rushmore heads were not. The Crazy Horse sculpture will show most of the man and the horse. The Rushmore figures show just the heads. Also, the Crazy Horse sculpture will be about 10 times larger than the Rushmore heads.

3. Answers will vary. There are two main reasons: the American government badly mistreated the Indians; Ziolkowski knew, from working with Borglum, that government promises of money were often delayed for years. He didn't want to have to put up with that.

4. Answers will vary. Today, there is a widespread desire to emphasize the diversity of those who have contributed to American life.

5. Answers will vary.

6. Answers will vary.

7. Answers will vary. Perhaps Ziolkowski felt that it was his destiny to carve this statue. Some people interpret coincidence as evidence that fate controls our lives.

HISTORY IN STONE

Making Inferences, page 68

1. True. Erosion is a continuing, slow process.
2. False. The Indian tribes lived far away from each other. They could not have been neighbors and friends.
3. False. He was very brave for navigating the river.
4. True. There is a gas station in the watchtower.
5. True. Fossils of underwater creatures have been found.

Practicing Vocabulary, page 68

1. erosion
2. barrier
3. fossils
4. rapids
5. waterfalls

Talking It Over, page 69

1. Lists will vary, but list (1) should include outdoor equipment and sturdy, casual clothing. List (2) can include

any of the tourist attractions mentioned in the chapter or others you might know of from experience.

2. Answers will vary. Many people's cultural traditions and religions prohibit polygamy. However, this practice is accepted in certain other cultures in Africa and Asia.

3. Answers will vary.

4. Yes, he cared about nature. Both the Grand Canyon and the Petrified Forest became protected areas when he was president.

5. Common superstitions are: walking under ladders, fear of black cats, and fear of the number *13*. Superstitions connected with luck are knocking on wood and finding a four-leaf clover, etc. Some superstitions are inherited from family members or are acquired from experience. Typical reasons for inventing superstitions might be: to prevent someone or something from harm, to assure safe passage, to gain luck, or to control one's fate.

DISNEY'S WORLD

Making Inferences, page 82

1. False. Fireworks, electric lights, and lasers brighten the night sky.

2. False. It takes at least a day to see each park.

3. False. It is the main launching station for NASA.

4. True.

5. False. It has many practical uses, such as weather forecasting, communications, and scientific research.

Practicing Vocabulary, page 82

1. guide
2. imagination
3. astronaut, blast
4. satellite
5. nutrition
6. earth
7. producer, adventure

Talking It Over, page 83

1. Some of the themes are Disney cartoon characters, Disney movies, science and technology, the future, American history, and the value of imagination.

2. Answers will vary.

3. Answers will vary. Here's some typical advice: Try to go at a less popular time to avoid large crowds. Wear comfortable

shoes because you'll do a lot of walking. Keep a careful eye on your belongings. Bring enough money to buy food and drinks frequently. You'll get hungry and thirsty often.

4. Answers will vary. Some well-known trademarks are *Coke*, *Xerox*, *Kleenex*, and many other brand-name products.

5. Most people would agree that it is a good investment. There are many benefits in the areas of communication and weather forecasting. There are also scientific experiments going on in zero gravity that may eventually improve medical care and improve life in other ways. Moreover, the space program satisfies a basic human need: to continue to explore new frontiers and try to change and improve the quality of life for people and other living things on earth.